SHAPES to CUT
Animals

Illustrated by Gary Mohrman

Teaching & Learning Company

1204 Buchanan St., P.O. Box 10
Carthage, IL 62321-0010

Table of Contents

Bear	5	Hippopotamus	19
Cat	6	Horse	20
Chicken	7	Lion	21
Cow	8	Monkey	22
Crow	9	Mouse	23
Dog	10	Ostrich	24
Donkey	11	Parrot	25
Duck	12	Pig	26
Elephant	13	Rabbit	27
Frog	14	Seal	28
Gila Monster	15	Sheep	29
Giraffe	16	Snake	30
Goat	17	Whale	31
Gorilla	18	Zebra	32

Cover by Gary Mohrman

Copyright © 1998, Teaching & Learning Company

ISBN No. 1-57310-132-X

Printing No. 98765

Teaching & Learning Company
1204 Buchanan St., P.O. Box 10
Carthage, IL 62321-0010

The purchase of this book entitles teachers to make copies for use in their individual classrooms only. This book, or any part of it, may not be reproduced in any form for any other purposes without prior written permission from the Teaching & Learning Company. It is strictly prohibited to reproduce any part of this book for an entire school or school district, or for commercial resale.

All rights reserved. Printed in the United States of America.

How to Use This Book

The patterns in this book provide simple shapes with round corners, thick lines, gentle angles and useful images for your children's first cutting experiences. Use the shapes individually to enhance a learning center or unit or use them in combination to create lively learning experiences.

It is usually easier if the children color the picture first and then cut it out. Some interesting effects can be achieved by having the children color white paper with markers (crayons and watercolors not recommended) and then copying the image onto the colored paper. If you do not want the children to color the picture, then you might copy it onto colored paper.

color shape   marker paper   colored paper

Other ideas include:
- tracing the picture onto thin interfacing (found in fabric stores) and coloring with marker. These make wonderful flannel board items.
- cutting the pattern out of tagboard or plastic (large ice cream container lids work well, check your school cafeteria) and using as a stencil.
- cutting the pattern out of a sponge and using for sponge painting.

Some things you can make with these patterns:

Puffy Stuff

Make fronts and backs. Before gluing shut, fill with a small amount of cotton batting or paper towel.

Flash Cards

Write beginning sounds or other facts on the shapes, use for review.

Mobiles
Make fronts and backs and hang from a coat hanger with string or yarn.

Stick Puppets
Attach a craft stick to the back and use to tell a story.

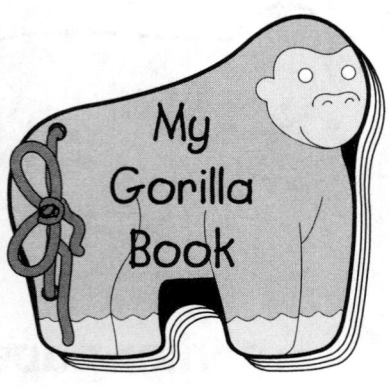

Shape Books

Some more things you can make with these patterns:
- bulletin board displays, door decorations, window decals
- name tags or place cards
- stationery
- portfolio covers or report covers
- flannel board pieces (cut from flannel or interfacing)
- gift wrap (cut from sponge and dip in tempera paint for sponge painting)
- stand-up figures (Make a front and back and glue together. Stand up with a small amount of clay.)
- sorting materials (Copy onto colored paper. Make sure you have at least two of the items in the same color. Cut out. Have children sort by color, shape, etc.)

You'll find many creative uses for the patterns in this book, and your young children will love having a collection of shapes to cut!

Lacing Items
Cut pattern from felt, glue two or three thicknesses together for strength. Use a hole punch to make holes around the edges about 1" (2.5 cm) apart. Supply blunt plastic needle and length of yarn.

Bear

Cat

Chicken

Cow

Crow

Dog

Donkey

11

Duck

Frog

Gila Monster

Goat

Gorilla

Hippopotamus

Horse

Lion

21

Monkey

Mouse

Ostrich

Parrot

Pig

Rabbit

Seal

Sheep

Snake

Zebra